SUPPORTING
BEHAVIOUR
IN THE CLASSROOM

SUPPORTING BEHAVIOUR IN THE CLASSROOM

{ Fintan O'Regan }

SAGE Publications Ltd
1 Oliver's Yard
55 City Road
London EC1Y 1SP

CORWIN
A SAGE company
2455 Teller Road
Thousand Oaks, California 91320
(0800)233-9936
www.corwin.com

SAGE Publications India Pvt Ltd
B 1/I 1 Mohan Cooperative Industrial Area
Mathura Road
New Delhi 110 044

SAGE Publications Asia-Pacific Pte Ltd
3 Church Street
#10-04 Samsung Hub
Singapore 049483

Editor: Delayna Spencer
Senior assistant editor: Catriona McMullen
Production editor: Nicola Carrier
Copyeditor: Sharon Cawood
Proofreader: Emily Ayers
Indexer: Gary Kirby
Marketing manager: Dilhara Attygalle
Cover design: Wendy Scott
Typeset by: C&M Digitals (P) Ltd, Chennai, India
Printed in the UK

**Library of Congress Control Number:
2020938049**

**British Library Cataloguing in
Publication data**

A catalogue record for this book is
available from the British Library

ISBN 978-1-5297-1855-3 (pbk)

This book is dedicated to all the students and colleagues that I have worked with over the years and from whom I have learned everything that is in this book.

I would also like to dedicate the book to the patience and expertise of my editor at SAGE who was outstanding in helping to translate all my thoughts and ideas into this finished resource that we trust will greatly support behaviour for learning.

TABLE OF CONTENTS

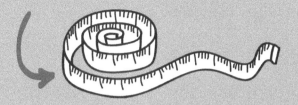

{ ABOUT THIS BOOK }

A Little Guide for Teachers: Supporting Behaviour in the Classroom inspires you to rethink how you manage behaviour. Using the author's tried and tested approach, this book encourages you to manage mood as a preventative strategy for disruptive behaviour.

- Authored by an expert in the field
- Easy to dip in-and-out of
- Interactive activities encourage you to write into the book and make it your own
- Fun engaging illustrations throughout
- Read in an afternoon or take as long as you like with it!

Find out more at
www.sagepub.co.uk/littleguides

a little guide for teachers

{ ABOUT THE SERIES }

A LITTLE GUIDE FOR TEACHERS series is little in size but big on all the support and inspiration you need to navigate your day-to-day life as a teacher.

 CASE STUDY

 HINTS & TIPS

 REFLECTION

 RESOURCES

 NOTE THIS DOWN

ABOUT THE AUTHOR

Fintan O'Regan works both nationally and internationally as a Behaviour and Learning Consultant and Trainer.

He was the head teacher of the Centre Academy from 1996 to 2002, which was the first international specialist school in the UK for students aged 7–19, specialising in issues related to learning behaviours.

He is an associate lecturer for Leicester University, the National Association of Special Needs, the Institute of Education, the Helen Arkell Dyslexia Centre and the former Vice Chairman of the UK ADHD Network.

He has written a number of books and published articles on the subject of learning, behaviour and socialisation issues. Fintan now works as a trainer and consultant for schools and school support systems, including social services, health, the police and foster carers, with regards to providing behaviour management strategies for children and families struggling with SEND and behavioural issues.

Author's website: www.fintanoregan.com

INTRODUCTION

I have always been interested in behaviour, in particular the connection between nature and nurture. When I started teaching Science in a secondary school, I quickly understood it wasn't just about teaching a subject, it was about understanding people. As a result, I suppose what really caught my fascination wasn't so much the students that learned how to behave in class, but the ones who didn't.

From there, I went down the SEND and behaviour route, eventually becoming head teacher of an international specialist school, where I came to understand different learning and behaviour styles.

For the last 15 years, I have been a behaviour and learning consultant. This book is a summary of many of the things that I have learned from the students and colleagues I have had the very great privilege of working with on this journey.

This book may contradict your views, confirm them or provide a totally new insight into supporting students in school.

Enjoy the journey.

CHAPTER 1
WHAT DOES BEHAVIOUR MEAN TO YOU?

This chapter provides an introduction to the concept of behaviour and demystifies it as a message from a child, who first needs to be understood before you can offer the most effective response. The chapter:

- Provides definitions of behaviour
- Outlines risk factors at school or at home which can negatively affect behaviour
- Covers understanding behaviour as a message from a child.

'The problem is the problem, not the child.'
Long, 2016

According to the Oxford English Dictionary, the word 'behaviour' is a noun defined as 'the way in which one acts or conducts oneself, especially towards others'. I would have thought it was more likely to be a verb, but then again this is the irony of the term. Despite being a word used by many of us on a regular basis, especially working within schools, it appears to me that it is a word that many people do not understand at all.

Consider the following conversation between two teachers at a recent staff meeting:

Teacher 1   'Jason is a real pain in the neck, he is always interrupting me and distracting the other students.'

Teacher 2   'Jason's really come a long way in my class and is always keen to contribute. I wish some of the others were as keen as him.'

These two statements are about the same student, but offer differing perspectives. Why does one person find Jason's 'behaviour' annoying, while the other person finds it interesting? It seems that Jason is capable of being a good student, but one teacher does not see this side of him. Although people would agree that specific behaviours such as aggression or acting out in the classroom are never appropriate, it does appear that attitudes towards what we might describe as low-level disruption differ from person to person.

Some people would say that children's behaviour is getting worse and will have an opinion on why that is, whether it's issues at home, the internet, not getting enough nutrition, and so on. Yet, there is no way to know if this is true. In this book, I would like to explore what we mean by behaviour and provide a process for how we meet its challenges.

 REFLECTION

What do you understand behaviour to mean? Are there any justifiable reasons for behaviour being considered as 'bad'?

DEFINITIONS OF BEHAVIOUR

Until very recently, the term used to describe behaviour issues in school was SEBD which stood for 'social, emotional and behavioural difficulties'. This term had evolved from the term EBD: 'emotional and behavioural difficulties'. To this day, some specialist schools are still referred to as EBD schools. In 2016, in the wake of the revised SEND Code of Practice, the term SEBD was revised to SEMH – social, emotional and mental health. This suggests a movement away from describing behaviourally challenged individuals towards a position that looks at the reasons or possible causes of why some individuals are more at risk than others when it comes to behavioural difficulties.

MENTAL HEALTH ISSUES

Until recently, people appeared reluctant to talk about the mental health of children, believing it to be something discussed among adults only. Yet, the reality is that just as we need to take care of children's physical health, we also need to take care of their mental health, no matter their age. A recent report entitled 'Mental Health and Behaviour in Schools', conducted by the Department of Education (2018), stated that 9.8% of children and young people aged 5–16 have a clinically diagnosed mental disorder. Within this group, 5.8% of all children have a conduct disorder (this is about twice as common among boys as girls), 3.7% have an emotional disorder, 1.5% a hyperkinetic disorder, and a further 1.3% have other, less common disorders, including autistic spectrum disorder, tic disorders, eating disorders and mutism (see Figure 1.1).

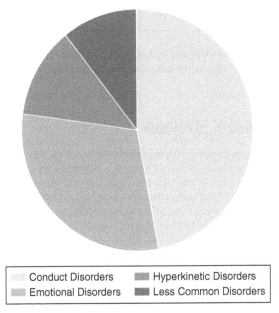

Conduct Disorders   Hyperkinetic Disorders
Emotional Disorders   Less Common Disorders

Figure 1.1   Clinically diagnosed mental disorders

1.9% of all children (approximately one fifth of those with a clinically diagnosed mental disorder) are diagnosed with more than one of the main categories of mental disorder. Beyond the 10% discussed above, approximately a further 15% have less severe problems which put them at increased risk of developing mental health problems in the future.

The report helpfully outlines four areas of risk factors that can increase the chances of a child developing mental health issues: risk factors in the child, in the family, in the community, and at school.

Risk factors in the child include:

- Specific learning difficulties/neurological difficulties
- Difficult temperament
- Levels of intelligence, IQ and EI
- Socialisation difficulties
- Physiological issues of levels of self-esteem, depression, stress
- Other health factors.

Risk factors in the family include:

- Overt parental conflict and family breakdown
- Sibling rivalry
- Inconsistent or unclear discipline
- Hostile or rejecting relationships
- Health of parents
- Failure to adapt to a child's changing needs
- Physical, sexual or emotional abuse
- Parental criminality, alcoholism or personality disorder
- Death and loss, including loss of friendship.

Risk factors in the community include:

- Socioeconomic disadvantage
- Homelessness
- Disaster, accidents, war or other overwhelming events
- Discrimination
- Other significant life events.

Risk factors at school include:

- Bullying

- Discrimination

- Breakdown in or lack of positive friendships

- Deviant peer influences

- Peer pressure

- Poor pupil and teacher relationship.

HINTS & TIPS: PROTECTIVE FACTORS FOR DEALING WITH RISK

For each of the four areas of risks factors, protective factors have been listed to allow you to better safeguard your children (see DfE, 2015).

All of the listed risk factors can have a significant influence on the development and SEMH of a child. This is not the first time risk factors have been outlined in this way, especially in terms of the individual, the family and the community. However, the one new area added to the spectrum in this report is risk factors in school.

Issues in school such as peer pressure, friendships and bullying are not new; however, the added pressure of cyber bullying means that children can no longer avoid the pressure of peers once they have left the school gates. I have heard it said on more than one occasion that the main reason why children WANT to go to school is not to learn or because we adults make them, but to see their friends. If friendships are something that a child finds challenging, or if they fear their peers, then their mental health and behaviour will be affected.

HINTS & TIPS: HOW CAN YOU SPOT MENTAL HEALTH ISSUES IN A CHILD?

Look out for ...

- **Poor eye contact**

- **Problems with communication**

- **Becoming easily frustrated and quick to anger**

- **Tardiness**

- **Over familiarity with adults**

- **Feigning sickness to avoid certain activities**

- **Lack of empathy.**

If you feel a child in your class is experiencing any of the above, talk to your safeguarding officer and engage the school SENCo.

RESOURCES

Your own mental health is important too, and in order to support your children to the best of your ability, you also need to look after yourself.

If you feel yourself experiencing mental health issues, try these resources for teachers:

www.educationsupport.org.uk/teachers-mental-health

www.bbc.co.uk/teach/teacher-support/new-mental-health-and-wellbeing-support-for-teachers/z4g4scw

DEMYSTIFYING BEHAVIOUR

When I began my career in teaching, the people who tended to study and write about behaviour were academics and psychologists. No one looking at behaviour in that time was applying it to the context of the classroom. It was with great relief that I discovered an Australian teacher called Bill Rogers who completely transformed the way I thought about and practised behaviour management. From attending his seminars (Rogers, 1997), I learned the following:

- Behaviour is learned.

- Behaviour is purposeful in a social setting.

- Behaviour is chosen.

- Behaviour communicates information about needs.

- Behaviour can be the result of BDS.

- Behaviour can be changed.

- Behaviour can be taught.

While the validity of these points can be debated, they gave me a great foundation upon which to build my own understanding of behaviour. Over time, I came to find that I disagreed with the idea that 'behaviour is chosen'. While in some cases this may be true, there are often times when it isn't. Some children who act in a disruptive way will often have acted completely without thinking. I call this 'non-premeditated behaviour'. The key question to consider when a child acts in a disruptive way, is whether or not they were in control of their actions. One of the statements listed by Rogers that I do strongly agree with is 'behaviour communicates information about needs'. As teachers, this is an important thing to understand. Behaviour does not occur in a vacuum; it is often in response to something. A child may have trouble with articulating their needs through words and it may come out in ways that disturb the classroom. The most effective way to support a child is to speak to them and understand where their actions are coming from. You can then put measures in place to prevent these actions from happening or support the child when they do.

The term BDS was a complete mystery to every person in the room and after a few incorrect guesses from individuals in the room it was revealed that the term stood for Bad Day Syndrome with the inference that some behaviour was simply a result of a person having a bad day.

For me however the term meant so much more as we were saying that behaviour is connected to a person's mood. Therefore I thought if you were able to influence and manage mood maybe you could support positive behaviour outcomes.

Finally I totally agreed with the statements behaviour could be changed and it could be taught.

 ## CASE STUDY

During one of my lessons, a 14-year-old student called Jack was in a bad mood. I saw him glaring at another child called Toby who was sitting at the desk in front of him. Ten minutes into the lesson, Jack kicked Toby's chair from underneath him and fists started flying.

I immediately stepped between them and told Jack to stand outside, while I moved Toby to a corner of the room. I went outside to speak to Jack who was pacing up and down the corridor. When I asked him what had happened, he told me Toby had been rude about his mother in the last class and that he was going to get him for it.

'No, you're not', I said. 'Even though you're upset, this stops now. I will deal with this behaviour at lunchtime when you both come to see me. You are both responsible for this situation and there will be further consequences if it continues. Do you understand?'

Consequences do often have traction for premeditated behaviour but less so for non-premeditated or impulsive behaviour. By the time you've considered what you've done, the action has already happened. In retrospect, I should have talked to Jack when he first came in and before the incident escalated. When it was happening, I didn't think I had time but, actually, by not interceding early enough I spent a lot more time later sorting out the incident.

Now that we have established a way of better understanding behaviour, next comes the task of being able to support it within the classroom and the school community. All schools will have policies on behaviour, safeguarding, bullying, and so on. However, in this book I outline an approach that I have developed over the years, through working with a range of different schools and school systems, called SF3R: structure, flexibility, rapport, relationships and resilience. Each of these terms acts as a vital cog in driving the behaviour management machine. Here I'll provide a short introduction, while later chapters will go into it in greater detail:

1.   Structure: this in essence provides the values, rules and systems that children and young people need in order to make sense of the world around them. Structure allows children and young people to feel safe and stable, and creates security in their lives. It also means developing clear boundaries and expectations and requires consistency in order to be effective.

2.   Flexibility: this is where adaptation to a range of different circumstances will complement the structure in our lives. Flexibility, when applied successfully, will allow freedom, opportunity and fun for all involved. Flexibility requires an appreciation of different people and cultures. It is inclusive and is based around equity rather than equality.

The 3Rs are the means of sustaining the long-term success of structure and flexibility:

1.   Rapport: this requires people skills, including the effective use of praise and the power of active listening. Successful rapport results in trust and respect for people for who they are and not who we wish them to be. Rapport creates respect, trust and self-esteem between people.

2.   Relationships: these are the lifelines for human beings to connect with each other in order to make sense of the world around them. Relationships allow you to form partnerships with people which are positive and productive.

3.   Resilience: this is a necessary quality for all teachers, allowing you to move on when something doesn't go your way. Resilience does not happen overnight or by chance; it requires a level of confidence that in many cases needs to be nurtured through effective structure and flexibility.

In practice, SF3R is not a formula, but more of a philosophy about how to support positive moods and therefore behaviour.

Chapters 3–5 provide specific examples of how and what each of these areas can look like in practice, but for now let's consider why these five words are vital in achieving behavioural management success.

CONCLUSION

In this first chapter, we have established that behaviour is a form of communication or a message that needs to be understood in order to best provide the appropriate support.

Although most behaviour is owned by a person, some students may not be choosing to make good choices regarding their behavioural actions, particularly if they have mental health issues.

Our role is to guide students to make better choices and provide systems that create consistency across a school, which should enable these choices to be made in a safe and structured environment. There will be times when things don't go according to plan, which is why we need to get technical about not managing behaviour but managing mood.

NOTE IT DOWN

Looking at the following statements, do you agree, disagree or are you unsure about them? Mark appropriately and say why for each:

Behaviour is learned.

Behaviour is purposeful in a social setting.

Behaviour is chosen.

BEHAVIOUR COMMUNICATES INFORMATION ABOUT NEEDS.

BEHAVIOUR CAN BE THE RESULT OF BDS.

BEHAVIOUR CAN BE CHANGED.

BEHAVIOUR CAN BE TAUGHT.

CHAPTER 2
HOW WELL CAN I MANAGE THE MOOD?

It's not behaviour management we do, it's mood management. This chapter will outline how managing the mood is one of the most effective ways of managing difficult, disruptive and defiant situations. This chapter:

- Helps you to understand the factors that affect mood
- Shows you how to apply mood management in practice
- Looks at the term reasonable adjustments within the school community.

'Don't be the drain, be the radiator.'

MOOD MANAGEMENT IN PRACTICE

In my training, rather than thinking of what we do as 'behaviour management' I talk about 'mood management'. Mood management is something that allows you to prevent situations escalating, by encouraging you to identify the moods around you and keep an eye on or deal with any moods that may lead to disruption. Within the classroom, there are three moods to consider:

1.   The mood of the teacher

2.   The mood of the student who may be having difficulties

3.   The mood of the other children in the classroom.

Before we look in depth at the first two points, let me start by considering the final point of the three listed.

In every classroom that I visit with regards to my consultancy, I am generally asked to consider one or two children. Once I have observed the class, I oftentimes report not only on the students identified, but also on two or three others who contribute to the original child's behaviour. The original child may or may not be acting in a premeditated way. However, the children I have identified as having a direct effect on the original child are choosing how they behave. These children I call the players. Often, it is boredom which leads them to negatively impact the behaviour of the original student – targeting another student is often a great distraction from the lesson, but there are ways to mitigate this, such as seating plans.

IDEAS FOR THE CLASSROOM
SEATING PLANS

There are many theories about seating plans and how best to set them up, but, to some extent, whether you set seats out in rows, in a horseshoe or something else, you will have to work within the confines of the shape and size of your classroom and, to some extent, the furniture you inherit.

You need to experiment with what you feel works best for you and your class. The jury is still out in terms of conflicting research on who should sit next to whom. Though it may be tempting to spread the nosier ones across the class, instead of having them in one location, they may just shout across the room instead of in a localised region.

My best tip is to sit children next to their friends rather than their peers. Having said that, they need to earn the right to stay there, and if it is not working then switch it. It is your classroom seating plan, not theirs.

THE MOOD OF THE TEACHER

It is always important to consider your own mood, as this can be vital to determining the climate and culture of the classroom. When we are in a good mood, we can handle everything and anybody, but we all know that things are not this easy if our mood is low. When we are in a bad mood, we are at risk of saying things we don't mean in the classroom. It is also possible that the players in the room may sense your bad mood and act upon this. I would argue that your mood is the most important in the classroom, as you are the person whose job it is to think about and protect any negative moods in order to facilitate learning.

When I talk about being in a 'good mood', I don't necessarily mean being overly enthusiastic or extremely happy (although it's always great to feel these things!). A good mood for a teacher is about being calm, measured and understanding. When we are in an aeroplane, we are told that if the cabin was to depressurise we would have to put on our own breathing masks before we help the children with theirs. Why? Because if the adult is able to breathe properly, he or she can best assist the children. I would argue that it is the same with mood management.

Liz Miller, in her book *Mood Mapping* (2011), has taken the issue of considering mood to a new level in terms of understanding, protecting and learning how to manage your own mood. She claims that anxiety, depression, calm and action are the four key moods that we exhibit.

There is no doubt that when you are relaxed you tend to be more in control and perhaps more patient with a student who is calling out all the time, while if you feel time-pressured or stressed you may feel less patient with your class. At the start of each day, before you start interacting with your class, you need to pause and ask yourself what sort of mood you are in. Checking in with yourself and recognising your own mood will help you to prepare for the rest of your day.

There are a number of factors which are responsible for determining your mood at any given point in time:

- The physical surroundings

- Your own wellbeing

- Connection with others

- Knowing your students

- Your attitude to situations.

You may want to consider which of the issues in the above list most affects your ability to stay focused and in control.

HINTS & TIPS: HOW TO SHUT OFF OUTSIDE DISTRACTIONS TO ALLOW YOU TO TEACH ON THE DAY

- Carry a card or have 4–5 inspirational statements on your phone to get you into teacher mode, for example 'Teaching isn't the filling of a pail, it's the lighting of a fire'.

- See every lesson as an opening-night performance.

- You only get one chance in life to be a Year 3 student.

- You will never ever have this time again … ever.

- You are a magnificent teacher and leader of the classroom.

YOUR OWN WELLBEING

It is important that you maintain good health and you owe it to yourself and your students to take charge of this. Teaching tests your energy levels and in order to maintain the standards required 190 days a year, this is a vital area to consider. Make time for yourself and do stuff that makes you feel happy and motivated.

HINTS & TIPS: LOOKING AFTER YOUR OWN WELLBEING

- Exercise: Walk instead of using the car or bus, join a gym, or do a local park run on Saturday mornings.

- Food and drink: Don't focus on what it tastes like; focus on how it makes you feel afterwards.

(Continued)

- **Sleep: Get your fair share of sleep and try to practise good sleep hygiene – try having some time before you go to sleep when you are not looking at a screen.**

- **Sensory stuff: Play the guitar, stroke the cat, and get the smelly candles out at bath time.**

- **Date night: make time to have one with a partner or a friend.**

CONNECTION WITH OTHERS

This is not just about your relationship with your students but also with colleagues, friends and family. We all have personal lives, and issues with our partners or family members can take over. It is inevitable that bad things will happen in our lives, but, to some extent, once you enter the classroom, you are on stage in front of your students and anything that detracts from your performance must be left behind or pushed to one side. Equally, a toxic school environment can really affect our emotions.

Athletes often talk about being 'in the zone' when they are competing. This essentially means that in order to achieve a great performance they must be totally focused on the moment of the activity to achieve a certain level of output. As a teacher, it is somewhat the same. You have to get yourself in the zone to deliver the lesson and provide the best possible outcome for your students. That means total focus on the subject and the students. Live in the moment!

KNOWING YOUR STUDENTS

They say knowledge is power, and understanding or broadening your knowledge about how or why your students act in certain ways, is vital to supporting them. For example, some individuals with ASD may avoid eye contact most of the time, especially when stressed or anxious. Without an understanding of this, it is easy to think they might not be paying attention and make the situation worse by telling them to listen to you. But having an understanding of the condition and its traits may help to de-escalate situations like this and allow you to provide more effective mood management.

YOUR ATTITUDE

Some people are more upbeat or energetic than others and the key is not to emulate them but to be yourself and to know your own nature. Having said that, students will be reading your mood, and some might be trying to deliberately make it worse, especially if you are already in a bad mood. If you are in a bad mood, try to manage it before you go into the classroom by working out a method that suits you.

THE MOOD OF A STUDENT HAVING DIFFICULTIES

Now let's look at the mood of the individual and how to work with that.

Early on in my career, I supervised a mock Maths exam. As I was walking around the room, I heard a loud scratching sound in the hall. After some investigation, I was surprised to find a student scratching on his desk with a compass. Knowing that he was disturbing the other students, I asked him to put the compass down, only to be ignored. I repeated the request, only for him to shout, 'Go away!'. Nothing in my teacher training had prepared me for that.

When my colleague saw what was going on, he started to walk over to the student, without any sense of urgency, making me feel extremely irritated and confused. He walked past me, without a word, and quietly spoke with the student.

'Hi Darren', he said, without any eye contact. 'Are you having a bad day? I thought you liked Maths?' Darren did not respond. 'You know, Darren, I have known this table here for five years. Now when I first came to this school this was the first table I remember sitting at. I love this table, Darren.' *What on earth is he doing?* I thought to myself. But I noticed Darren's mouth twitch. He was smiling. My colleague noticed this too and asked Darren if he wanted to go for a walk. Darren got up, leaving the compass on the table and walked out of the room quietly.

After the exam, I sought out my colleague to ask how he had managed the situation. He said, 'Darren's dead good at sums but he can't read the bloody questions.'

It is really important to know if any of your students have reading difficulties, not just for English or subjects with a high word content such as history, but for all subjects. This incident occurred some time ago, when we had less of an understanding about dyslexia. Had Darren been taking the test today, provisions would be made to help him cope with the questions. Although Darren's actions and disruptions were not justified, we can understand more about his frustrations and, as a result of this, in future exam situations we were able to give Darren some additional support in reading.

Three key points can be seen in this account:

1.   Behaviour is a message.

2.   If you can change mood in the first instance, this will help to diffuse the situation and affect behaviour.

3.   You own your own behaviour.

The first two points have been the major focus of this chapter, while the third point will be one of the key issues covered in Chapter 3.

CONCLUSION

During a staff meeting at a school where I was head teacher, I heard two teachers having an interesting discussion about one student. While one member of staff described him as annoying and always shouting out, another found him overenthusiastic, always keen to contribute to the lesson. The student in question was doing the same thing in each class, but the attitude towards him varied. To some extent, particularly with low-level behaviour, the attitude of the teacher determines how disruptive it is to the class. As a result, while behaviour can be an abstract term, mood is clear and concise, which is why managing and supporting mood can be seen as a more practical and positive approach.

NOTE IT DOWN

THINK OF THREE ISSUES OR SITUATIONS THAT PUT YOU IN A
BAD MOOD IN THE CLASSROOM AND WRITE THEM DOWN ON A
PIECE OF PAPER. FOR EACH OF THEM, CONSIDER:

HOW DOES THIS AFFECT YOU?

HOW DOES IT AFFECT OTHERS?

WHAT DO YOU DO ABOUT IT NOW?

DOES IT CHANGE THINGS AND WHY OR WHY NOT? IF NOT, DISCUSS WHAT YOU COULD DO DIFFERENTLY.

NOW, ON A DIFFERENT SHEET OF PAPER, WRITE DOWN THREE THINGS THAT PUT YOU IN A GOOD MOOD:

1. TAKE A PICTURE OF THE SHEET AND KEEP IT IN YOUR PHONE.

2. MAKE THE SHEET OF PAPER INTO A PAPER AEROPLANE.

3. LAUNCH YOUR PAPER AEROPLANE ACROSS THE ROOM.

CHAPTER 3
STRUCTURE

In this chapter, we consider the learning climate, including why setting boundaries and expectations allows students to feel safe and secure. This chapter:

- Explains why a child needs to understand that they are responsible for their own actions
- Explores reasonable adjustments which may be needed to be made by the student
- Details different teaching styles.

Children need to understand that they are responsible for their own actions. If a child grows up with the idea that they are not responsible for their actions, then there is a chance that they may always be in denial and will not accept being held to account by others. The key is helping individuals to take responsibility for their actions and for them to understand that they always have choices. However, if they make a choice that is deemed inappropriate, there will be consequences.

This is why schools have behaviour policies that provide a structure so that everyone can work and live together within a safe and secure community. As in all communities, there are rules by which people need to abide and, although not everyone will agree with the rules by common consent, they can choose to follow the rules or not.

Within school systems, this is where the term 'reasonable adjustments' has a role. A reasonable adjustment is presenting a student with the option to make a choice about actions or behaviours in specific situations. If a choice has not been provided, then, to some extent, a school could be in breach of both behaviour and/or SEN policies (where relevant). However, if a choice has been provided and a student makes the incorrect choice, then they are responsible for their own actions.

There is, however, so much more to structure than rules and boundaries. In essence, structure allows for the following:

1. Reduced anxiety

2. Enhanced motivation, confidence and self-esteem

3. Increased concentration through reducing distractions

4. Facilitating independence.

It is a myth that students or people who have behaviour issues dislike structure. It is actually the case that those that fight structure need it the most and deep down they know this, though often they would be loath to admit it. In my past role as a head teacher of an SEBD school (i.e. one for those with social, emotional and behavioural difficulties), whenever I interviewed students, the majority of whom had been either fixed term or permanently excluded from previous schools, I would ask them who was their favourite teacher. Most of them were somewhat disgruntled with the teachers they had known, yet after a while they would admit that there was one person who stood out from the rest. The characteristics of that person might be somewhat surprising. Generally, the teacher who they liked the most was someone who could handle the noisy kids, someone of whom they could say that you knew where you stood with them, and someone you could have a laugh with. What they were saying is that they liked best the teacher who had a clear and consistent structure by employing the rules fairly and consistently, and helped them to feel safe and secure in the classroom.

What I understood from these students is that they wanted someone who was in control of the class and could manage all of the students, making everyone adhere to the rules and routines. This may have included making sure no one was getting away with things or receiving special treatment. They also respected the fact that the teacher treated them as a human being and understood when to lighten the mood. When you have structure, it reduces anxiety by making people feel safe. This, in turn, allows for a climate of learning which allows individuals to express themselves in a positive and productive way.

IDEAS FOR THE CLASSROOM
HOW TO CREATE A POSITIVE ROUTINE

- **Meet and greet students at the door and be firm on punctuality.**

- **Make sure your room is clutter-free and that tables and chairs are where they should be, as you set the example of a tidy, structured environment.**

- **Set out the lesson objectives on the whiteboard.**

- **Appear positive and enthusiastic about the lesson, as you set the mood.**

(Continued)

- **Make sure everyone is clear about the method of asking questions and interacting with them.**

- **Make sure your exit is as formal as your start.**

TEACHING STYLES

All schools will have rules and woven into these will be behaviour policies. The main premise of rules is to establish an environment that is safe for everyone and which provides the optimum opportunities for productive learning. Policies are useful, but only to a point. What it is key to consider here are those people who are enforcing the rules and the ways in which they do it. Thus, your teaching style is essential to how you create structure within the classroom:

1. Your style affects the climate in the classroom.

2. Your style models the behaviour that children copy.

3. The beliefs that you hold determine your style of approach.

It has been said that there are three main teaching styles:

- The Controller

- The Friend

- The Benign Dictator.

Having been in many staff rooms over the years, I might add the Grumbler, the Optimist, the Competitive One, the Pacifist, the Chatterbox and the Explosive One. However, for now let's consider the characteristics of these three main types.

THE CONTROLLER

Attitude:

- Children should be seen and not heard.

- Don't smile till Christmas.

- If one person gets away with it, they will all do it.

- It's a battle and I aim to win it.

This is a kind of 'my way or the highway' approach.

Key strategies will be to:

- Tell children what to do

- Threaten them with consequences

- Send them to somebody else.

This is a blunt instrument approach with no plan B, which is why when it doesn't work other members of staff will need to be involved. The results will be as follows:

- Poor quality relationships

- High quality stress

- Learning and risk taking will be impaired.

This style is mainly about being in charge and enforcing power. It will not work for all students. The style also does not allow for children to be treated as individuals, as they are all treated in the same way. In direct contrast and at the other end of the spectrum, you have our next style: the Friend.

THE FRIEND

Attitude:

- Children need nurturing.

- Being nice and friendly means children will like you.

- Classrooms are a democracy where negotiation is the key.

- Planning excellent work will always be enough.

This individual wants to be liked by the students and believes that a caring, democratic and friendly approach will be appreciated.
Key strategies to achieve this will be:

- Asking, negotiating, pleading, followed by;

- 'Why are you doing this to me?' (hurt); and

- 'How many times have we been through this?' (frustration).

There will be some difficulties here as students don't want you as their friend; they have friends their own age sitting behind them. But they do need you as their teacher. The results will often be as follows:

- Uncertainty leads to insecurity.

- Learning is significantly impaired.

It is likely therefore that children want someone who they can feel safe with and who can provide a productive climate for learning. The final option is what I believe to be the best style: the Benign Dictator.

THE BENIGN DICTATOR

Attitude:

- A teacher's job is to set boundaries.

- A child's job is to test them.

- Children should be helped to experience achievement, and mistakes will be part of the journey.

- Caring means sometimes being prepared to make unpopular decisions.

- The problem is the problem, not the child.

- Fairness is not giving everybody the same; it is giving them what they need: equity rather than equality.

It might sound a bit severe, but in reality this is what is needed to own the room and facilitate learning. It is also critical that you learn to cope with the fact that not every child will like you; what you are after is their respect and you can achieve this by being consistent.

The last two bullet points are also very important as you will need to separate the child from the behaviour and understand that some children will need more time and possibly more flexibility than others.

Key strategies to achieve this will be:

- To hold children accountable for their choices

- To create a culture of praise that focuses on what children do well

- To redirect children towards success

- To apply consequences, positive and negative, with consistency.

As a result of this, the outcomes will be as follows:

- Children learn boundaries with dignity.

- The teacher is both leader and coach in the classroom.

- Learning, risk taking and motivation are greatly enhanced.

 REFLECTION

Of the three teaching styles, which one or parts of the three reflect your own practice?

What do you think you may want to do differently in order to improve your teaching style?

In order to help you consider how to apply this in practice, I want to describe a successful classroom strategy which was inspired by a former colleague. The second school I worked at was an independent school in the USA, full of highly motivated students. Having learned the basis of behaviour management in a challenging school in the UK, I thought that this would be a breeze. However, I was shocked to find that the general attitude towards teachers was highly negative and that students largely looked down on their teachers.

One weekend, after a particularly challenging week, I called a former colleague in Newcastle to ask for his advice. He told me that he was going to give me four pieces of advice that I would need to work out for myself. He said: 'get them in, get on with it, get on with them, and get them out.' Then the phone went dead. Stunned, I thought, what on earth was he talking about, and then it dawned on me that what he was saying was 'sort out your rituals, own the room and act like a Benign Dictator'.

The following is my outline for how you do this.

Get them in:

- Have you gone through your class rituals regarding dress code, bags, phones, food/drink, and so on?
- Can you arrange the seating plan to reduce potential trouble spots?
- Can you see your students at all times?
- Does your equipment work and do you have your materials in advance?

So, essentially, you are laying the groundwork for the class ahead and making sure you have ownership of the room in terms of the non-negotiables.

Get on with it:

- Make students active participants in the learning.
- Have a passion for your subject.
- Be well organised and monitor the pace.
- Give students feedback as quickly as possible.
- Work from the students' strengths and interests, i.e. focus on what they can do as opposed to what they can't do.
- Reward success.

Get on with them:

- Listen actively to what they say.

- Be assertive as opposed to aggressive.

- Strive for friendly and informed interactions.

- Be adaptable; if it's not working for them, then change your approach.

After the initial involvement in the work, inevitably some students will get bored or distracted by each other and that's when the fine-tuning of how you manage these situations will determine the climate of the class and the flow of the lesson.

Get them out:

- Have you left time for clearing up, setting homework, and so on?

- Are they ready to be released for the next lesson?

- Is anybody edgy, upset, angry? ... Read the mood.

- Is the room ready for the next set of students that will come in?

As vital as it is getting them in, make sure it's an ordered exit and not chaos in terms of students leaving the room by pushing people out of the way and having issues spilling into the corridor. Otherwise, you may ignite issues that colleagues in the next class inherit. And, by the way, it worked with my US class. Students all over the world respond to this approach because it's not about crowd control, it's about people management.

CONCLUSION

Developing a framework with boundaries and expectations is crucial. Policies and procedures are one thing but implementing them successfully requires people acting and reacting in specific ways and at specific times. In order to do this, you will also need to allow for a degree of flexibility and have boundaries that can stretch, because not everything goes to plan.

NOTE IT DOWN

Imagine your lesson is split into three parts: the start, the middle and the end.

Pre-Planning: What Will I Teach?

Many times, as busy teachers, we jump right into the planning stage of preparing a lesson, but skipping pre-planning can actually cost you more time in the long run. Pre-planning can be a great time to make decisions about the direction of your lesson.

Planning: How Will I Teach It?

Planning is when you answer the question of how you will accomplish your learning objectives. This includes deciding on and planning out your activities, lectures, group projects, homework, and so on. It may result in a formal lesson plan or simply a to-do list or course of action. How you decide to record your plan is up to you and the expectations you have to meet.

POST-PLANNING: WHERE WILL I GO NEXT?

POST-PLANNING REFERS TO THE TIME YOU COMMIT TO REFLECTING ON THE LESSON YOU TAUGHT, STRATEGISING BASED ON THAT LESSON, AND THINKING ABOUT THE UPCOMING CLASS.

HOW YOU LEARN FROM YOUR MISTAKES, REPLICATE YOUR VICTORIES AND STRATEGISE FOR YOUR NEXT CLASS IS UP TO YOU. POST-PLANNING GIVES YOU THE SPACE AND TIME TO LEARN FROM BOTH YOUR VICTORIES AND YOUR MISTAKES, WHICH IS AN INVALUABLE TOOL FOR BOTH YOU AND YOUR STUDENTS. AND, IF THINGS DIDN'T GO AS PLANNED DURING YOUR LESSON, WHAT CAN YOU LEARN FROM THIS?

WOULD THIS ABOVE APPROACH IMPROVE THE OUTCOME OF YOUR LESSONS?

OUTLINE SOME METHODS THAT YOU CAN RELY UPON TO KEEP THE ORDER IN EACH OF THESE SECTIONS.

CHAPTER 4
FLEXIBILITY

This chapter considers how teachers need to be adaptable and flexible as well as structured. This is because no two children will ever be the same and some will be more different than others. The term neuroflexibility is introduced to help us consider how the issue of fairness isn't giving everybody the same things, but giving each individual what they need. This chapter:

- Outlines how flexibility complements structure
- Explains the concept of neurodiversity and how to support traits and not labels
- Introduces neuroflexibility as a strategy of support.

'There is no such thing as dyslexic, ASD or ADHD children but there are some children with dyslexia, ASD or ADHD traits.'

As I've said previously, while structure and flexibility sound contradictory, they are actually complementary. Let me explain what I mean in terms of behaviour management.

Table 4.1 Comparison of Bands 1 and 2

Band 1	Band 2
Physical/verbal abuse	Distractibility
Bullying	Disorganisation
Using phones in class	Calling out
Chewing	Fidgeting
Dress code	Engaging others during class

In Table 4.1, I've outlined some generally agreed inappropriate behaviours. Band 1 outlines the key expectations and non-negotiables in a mainstream secondary school. These issues can easily be dealt with using the Benign Dictator/Get Them In approach. There is no room for discussion or compromise as these are the key expectations and rules for how the school runs.

Band 2 is where flexibility comes in. Understanding and accepting this will not be easy for every teacher, but the key is to accept that, within inclusive schools, not every student will be able to help themselves calling out, and not having a pen is not a crime against humanity.

CASE STUDY

Nathan was a bright but extremely disorganised 13-year-old who never seemed to have a pen nor any of his equipment when he arrived in my class. I had tried discipline for this by giving him detentions for lack of organisation, and even positives such as merits for when he brought all his equipment in, but nothing worked.

In a particular class when I was not in the best of moods myself, I asked the class to start working, only to see Nathan's hand shoot up: 'Can I borrow a pen, Sir?'

> 'Nathan, what have I told you before about not bringing a pen to class? You never bring a pen.'

> 'I had last time, Sir, do you remember you said well done', said Nathan with a smile.

> 'Well, you haven't got one today and you don't seem to care', I snapped back.

> Practically in tears, Nathan said to me, 'Why don't you keep one for me?'

Initially, I was shocked and taken aback for two reasons:

1. I didn't look as if I was giving in on the issue on behalf of the rest of the class.

2. It really wasn't such a bad idea but he had thought of it first.

From that the day forward, I kept a pen in my desk for Nathan, which he would borrow and return to me at the end of class. Not only were we both happier with this routine, but the rest of the class also responded well to the change. What this situation taught me is that fairness isn't treating everybody the same, it is giving each individual what they need. This was something that worked for Nathan.

 REFLECTION

In your own situation and based on the age of the children that you teach, what would be your Band 1 of non-negotiables versus Band 2 – those issues that you may be willing to be more flexible on?

Band 1: Non-negotiables	Band 2: Flexible areas

Would this banding conflict with other members of staff that you work with?

NEURODIVERSITY

Neurodiversity is a term which was first coined in the late 1990s to describe conditions such as autism (ASD), dyslexia and ADHD, not as deficits or disorders, but rather as variations or differences of the human brain. It emerged as a challenge to prevailing views that certain neurodevelopmental disorders are inherently pathological, and instead adopts the social model of disability, in which societal barriers are the main contributing factor that disable people.

For teachers in particular, attempting to run and organise a classroom with perhaps three or four students with mild to moderate traits of ASD or ADHD can pose a challenge in terms of being sensitive to the needs of students with such traits, while being conscious of the needs of the rest of the class.

In order to establish some clarity and consistency across the classroom, therefore, it is highly recommended that a Band 1 is established in terms of the structure that should be adhered to by everybody within the class.

However, shouting out of turn or fidgeting, although they may be annoying or irritating, may need to be understood as messages of how the child learns differently. SpLD, ASD and ADHD are neurodevelopmental differences and, as a result, children with these traits will stand out and be different from their peers; as such differences manifest themselves by exhibiting neurodevelopmental delay in specific age-related skill sets, they will need a greater degree of flexibility in Band 2. In other words, children with neurodiversity require neuroflexibility in terms of a behaviour management approach.

Every classroom is likely to have between 5% and 20% of children who have a range of neurodiverse differences, so the rigidity which sits within the Controller style of management discussed in the last chapter will lead to unsuccessful outcomes. I will briefly cover the key traits of SpLD, ASD and ADHD.

Specific learning difficulties (SpLDs), including dyslexia, dyscalculia and dyspraxia, usually result in impairments to some or all of the following:

- *Input*: visual perception/auditory perception
- *Integration*: sequencing, organisation, abstraction
- *Memory*: short term/long term
- *Output*: motor/oral.

This can lead to difficulties in some or all of these specific issues:

- Speed of processing
- Short-term memory

- Sequencing

- Auditory perception and processing

- Visual perception and processing

- Laterality difficulties

- Organisation

- Decoding written language.

 ## CASE STUDY

A student who I once knew with dyslexia, when taking her GCSEs, was told by her teacher that the effort that she and the rest of the class had put into it was like they were trying to swim the English Channel. The dyslexic student told her teacher: 'that might be true for the rest of the class, but for me it's like trying to swim the Channel but it's made of treacle and I have to put so much extra effort into every single stroke.'

 ## IDEAS FOR THE CLASSROOM
HOW TO OFFER NEUROFLEXIBILITY FOR STUDENTS WITH SPLDS

Provide students with SpLDs with arrangements that benefit them, such as:

- **A scribe, a prompter, a laptop or more time**

- **Standing tables versus sitting**

- **Toys to fiddle with when sitting and listening**

- **Movement breaks**

- **Work stations around the room**

- **The allowance to listen to music when working, either privately or within the group setting.**

AUTISM SPECTRUM DIFFERENCES

The three core traits are as follows:

- *Communication*: language impairment across all modes of communication – speech, intonation, gestures, facial expressions and other body language

- *Imagination*: rigidity and inflexibility of the thought process – resistance to change, obsessional and ritualistic behaviour

- *Socialisation*: difficulties with social relationships, poor social timing, lack of empathy, rejection of normal body contact, inappropriate eye contact.

These traits can lead to the following:

- Literal thinking

- Obsession with certain topics that leads to exceptional knowledge in one area

- Talking at another child rather than engaging in two-way conversation

- Excellent memory

- Difficulties with social interaction

- Poor motor co-ordination

- Difficulty in understanding and appreciating other people's feelings and perspectives

- Difficulty in reading social cues

- Little empathy for others.

CASE STUDY

On a recent visit to a school, I observed a 13-year-old student called Aditya, who had ASD, being introduced to the science teacher in one of the labs. The teacher asked Aditya if she liked science and she responded that she did and proceeded to tell him about all the practical work she had done and how she liked to make hydrogen pop with a flame. The teacher then asked her to name something that could be dangerous in a science lab. Rather than saying something obvious like an unsupervised flame, or spilling acids, Aditya responded confidently with, 'a motorbike'.

Aditya's answer was not wrong, and certainly creative; however, it wasn't what the teacher was looking for. Yet, if the teacher had a better understanding of autism, he would know that asking an open-ended question such as this to someone with a literal brain isn't the right way to achieve what he saw as the correct answer. In adopting a neuroflexible approach, he would have a better understanding of how to phrase his questions; it might also mean that he would praise the creativity of her answer.

IDEAS FOR THE CLASSROOM
HOW TO OFFER NEUROFLEXIBILITY FOR STUDENTS WITH ASD

For students with ASD:

- Provide an area in the class where the student can have their own space.

- Ensure elements of continuity and prepare students in advance for changes.

- Offer a visual task list where possible.

- Explain jokes, idioms and figures of speech.

- **Reduce distractions.**

- **Have a routine schedule.**

- **Have a place to take a break.**

- **Maintain consistency.**

- **Control background noise.**

- **Be aware of heightened sensitivity to sensory stimuli (including lights, sounds, smells and textures).**

ADHD

The three core traits here are:

- *Impulsivity*: being unable to regulate verbal or motor control

- *Inattentiveness*: having difficulty in sustaining attention

- *Hyperactivity*: excessive movement or hypo activity; excessive mental drifting.

These traits can lead to the student struggling with the following issues:

- Poor listening skills

- An inability to follow directions

- Poor organisation

- Being easily distracted

- Being forgetful

- A tendency to blurt out answers and interrupt others

- A failure to consider consequences

- Excessive fidgeting

- An inability to sit still

- Excessive talking

- Excessive movement.

The range of issues outlined above requires a flexible mindset. In my experience, it is often the adults leading the class that have the biggest issue with these students, as they can be hard to support, while the rest of the class just accepts it. They understand these students are different; they just aren't sure why.

 ## CASE STUDY

During a Year 8 science class, Sadiq, one of my top students, came up to me and said, 'Sir, you know David? He needs the magnets.' I was really puzzled. We had had a lesson on magnets two days ago and had now moved on to something else. I pointed this out to Sadiq, who repeated his former request: 'I know, Sir, but David needs the magnets.' Stepping back, I remembered that David, who had ADHD traits, was really a very active student who was usually fiddling or swinging on his chair during class and he had been fascinated by the magnets and extremely well behaved during the lesson. Sadiq wanted me to give David the magnets so he could fiddle selectively. The students had made their own assessment.

 ## IDEAS FOR THE CLASSROOM
HOW TO OFFER NEUROFLEXIBILITY FOR STUDENTS WITH ADHD

In terms of positioning:

- Try and work out what are the main distracters (auditory, visual, kinaesthetic, internal).

- Can you see the student(s) at all times?

- Reduce your expectations of seat work and use alternative ways of task completion.

In terms of studying:

- Give only one or two activities per page.

- Pair the child with strong role models (both academic and social).

- Use preferential seating arrangements.

In terms of supporting focus:

- Allow the student to fiddle with an agreed object, e.g. a stress ball, tangle toys.

- Give short breaks between assignments.

- Plan ahead for transition times.

- Use alternative technology, e.g. a computer, music.

- Set a variety of tasks and activities; where possible, include a 'hands-on' activity.

- Give the whole class stretching exercises midway through.

ODD

One term we haven't mentioned yet is oppositional defiant disorder or ODD. This describes a pattern of negativistic, hostile and defiant behaviour lasting at least six months, during which four or more of the following are present:

- Often loses temper

- Often argues with adults

- Often actively defies or refuses to comply with adults' requests or rules

- Often deliberately annoys people

- Often blames others for their mistakes or behaviour

- Is often touchy or easily annoyed by others

- Is often angry or resentful

- Is often spiteful and vindictive.

This is, in essence, an extreme case of pushing back at structure and any flexibility. This is basically saying, *I'm not buying what you are selling*. When in business you have a problem in selling, you need to get onto the marketing department who talk about using the 5Ps to get the sale done: Price, Promotion, Product, Place and People.

The first four of these, in theory, should already be active due to your structure and flexibility options in terms of classroom set-up and learning objectives, and rewards for compliance; the key component being *the people to get the message across*. People buy from other people, but in order to get them to do this you must gain their trust, which means building rapport, and this will be the starting point of the next chapter.

CONCLUSION

Being able to successfully apply flexibility within the structure means believing that fairness isn't giving everybody the same thing, but giving each person what they need.

With regards to neurodiversity, this means accepting that you will need to be adaptive in your approach and try different solutions to support that student in their learning. A quick solution to this would be to be proactive and contact the parent of that particular student so that you can find out a few methods from someone who knows them best.

NOTE IT DOWN

Think of a student and choose one key issue that is the major cause for concern:

In what situations does the issue occur (i.e. in what settings)?

In which situations does the issue not occur?

What view does the young person have of themselves regarding this issue?

What skills does the young person have (e.g. social/communication skills, learning/sporting/artistic skills)?

What message, in your opinion, is this student sending through their actions?

USING THE ABOVE LIST, NOW CONSIDER YOUR RESPONSE
BOTH IN THE SHORT TERM AS IN AN IMMEDIATE CLASSROOM
INTERVENTION, AND IN THE LONG TERM, PERHAPS INVOLVING
AN OUTSIDE AGENCY.

SHORT-TERM RESPONSE	LONG-TERM RESPONSE

CHAPTER 5
THE 3 Rs

This chapter explores the 3Rs (rapport, relationships and resilience) and will consider the art of effective communication along with positive relationships between teachers and students. This chapter:

- Shows you how to develop effective *rapport* with students
- Explores the power of *relationships* and rewards
- Looks at the importance of *resilience* and developing self-worth.

'It's not what you say, but how you say it.'

There is a song by the pop group *Fun Boy Three* which goes by the title 'It Ain't What You Do (It's The Way That You Do It)', and this could be the mantra for how you deliver structure and flexibility. Many young people with challenging behaviours have been battered and bruised by negativity and may have decided that the worst they can be is the best they can be. This is where the 3 Rs come in. This is not about dictating to a student or forcing them to conform; it is about earning and building a student's trust and confidence in you, so that they choose to work with you and not against you.

RAPPORT

Rapport derives from the Latin word 'rapportare', meaning to 'bring back'. As teachers, this is what we might need to do for those students who exhibit challenging behaviour – bring them back from making negative choices that can get them into trouble.

The modern-day definition for 'rapport' is 'a close and harmonious relationship in which the people or groups concerned understand each other's feelings or ideas and communicate well'. Communication is something we do every day, but there are ways that we can improve it to work for the individuals who need more within the classroom.

Albert Mehrabian (1971) defined communication as follows:

- 7% words

- 38% tonality, volume and tempo

- 55% non-verbal signals.

Mehrabian makes the point that the majority of communication is not about the words we use, but how those words are delivered. Maximum impact is gained by how the words are transmitted by the person. As a teacher, you know the importance of delivery; it is how you keep the students actively listening and engaged.

In terms of working with and supporting children with challenging behaviours, there are some steps that can be taken with regards to communication, such as:

- Using eye contact

- Being flexible at times

- Considering height/level positioning

- Appearing relaxed

- Nodding

- Being aware of personal space and balance

- Using facial expressions

- Not fidgeting yourself

- Being focused and using active listening.

The last point regarding listening is crucial. There are two main types of listening: (1) listening to reply; and (2) listening to understand. The latter is the most productive form of active listening as you are striving to really *hear* what a person is saying.

 # HINTS & TIPS: ACTIVE LISTENING

- **Give your complete focus to what the other person is saying.**

- **Let the other person finish before you start talking.**

(Continued)

- **Use eye contact where possible.**

- **Keep your emotions in check.**

- **Don't interrupt or jump to conclusions.**

- **Look for feelings or the intent behind the words.**

 # REFLECTION

What would you say have been the key issues in developing effective rapport with your students, and in particular how would you rate your listening skills?

Although words may only be 7% of communication, they are still extremely important and in certain situations it is vital you choose the correct ones. This would certainly be the case when working with students with ODD traits, mentioned at the end of the last chapter, who are likely to be extremely resistant in specific situations.

Students with this condition are highly sensitive to direction, especially in group situations involving peers, and the words that are used should be those that nudge and do not appear to nag for compliance. I have listed here some important sentence starters, particularly when starting conversations with disillusioned or reluctant learners:

- Let's…

- I need you to…

- In five minutes you will have…

- When I return I will see…

- Today we are going to…

- You will be…

- I expect you to…

- I know that you will…

- Thank you for…

I particularly like 'I need you to' as you are manoeuvring the student to make the decision and not telling them. It's also harder to argue against, as 'can you' or 'will you' could easily be met with 'no'. Creating a rapport is not always easy but it is vital in terms of employing structure and flexibility. Once established, you can then move on to the next level which is establishing positive relationships.

RELATIONSHIPS

Humans are driven towards forming relationships with other people, and indeed evolution of the human race is dependent on this. Schools are places where deep and meaningful relationships occur within a community that is unique to itself but similar to other schools in terms of the importance of those relationships.

As such, the three main sets of relationships that occur in school are:

- Student and teacher

- Peer to peer

- Teacher and teacher/staff.

In terms of student to teacher, we have already viewed the process of how this takes place and how students generally prefer the teacher to be their teacher and not a friend. As we know, a relationship is a two-way process and both parties need to work on it for a relationship to be successful. Obviously, the teacher is the key player in this relationship and will need to observe the key issues of structure and flexibility, but there is also the question of feedback to the student, which will usually involve rewards and sanctions.

Rewards and sanctions can moderate behaviour but they are usually only as effective as the delivery of them. Most children won't be happy with a sanction but they will usually accept them, reluctantly. However, they will not be accepted when the delivery of the sanction is given in a way that embarrasses or threatens the child, who may react badly.

Note the following key points:

- A reward is given as a result of a behaviour.

- A reward is given in recognition of a behaviour that is in the child's best interest.

- Sanctions will be something that children do not like but they should not be physically or psychologically harmful.

- Sanctions are a choice that children make.

- Sanctions do not have to be severe to be effective.

 # HINTS & TIPS: THINGS TO AVOID WHEN DELIVERING A SANCTION

When delivering a sanction, try NOT to:

- **Shout at the student**

- **Ignore their views**

- **Bring up past, unrelated misdemeanours other than the issue at hand**

- **Stand too close to the child**

- **Raise your voice in response to theirs in an attempt to be the loudest**

- **Allow conflict in a public forum**

- **Engage in hostile, non-verbal actions, such as arms flailing, aggressive facial expressions, and so on.**

Often, such actions will generate a fight or flight reaction in the student and are a precursor to anger.

REWARDS

Everybody likes rewards, be it stickers, house points, freedom of movement, and so on. But just as disappointment is the most effective sanction from someone whom you have a good relationship with, praise is the ultimate reward. I would argue that there is a science to praise as not everyone is able to accept or deal with it in the same way. Yet, praise can work to improve self-esteem, self-reliance, autonomy, achievement and motivation. It should be seen as encouragement and part of the continuous process of learning.

Relationships are the cornerstone of teaching. I will leave the final word to Sean Misteil (1997) on this who said:

We listen to those

We like and respect

We like and respect those with whom we can identify or identify with us

We pay attention to those whom we believe mean what they say.

RESILIENCE

Resilience is the last of the 3 Rs and involves three related elements:

- A sense of self-esteem and confidence

- A belief in one's own self-efficacy and the ability to deal with change and adaptation

- A repertoire of social problem-solving approaches.

For decades, resilience was seen as the ability to recover from disaster and hardship. Researchers focused on how people bounced back from tragedies like hurricane, fire and flood. They studied why some people get 'back to normal' quickly, while others continue to struggle.

Schools have typically viewed resilience in a similar way. They'd think of it in terms of how quickly the child bounced back from an illness, a learning difficulty or perhaps an incident involving bullying or unhappiness at school. In other words, resilience was something the child 'showed' when faced with a big challenge.

However, resilience has a much broader meaning – it's not just about 'bouncing back'; it's also about 'bouncing forward'. Resilience doesn't just mean getting back to normal after facing a difficult situation. It means learning from the process in order to become stronger and better at tackling the next challenge.

Using everyday setbacks to explore new and better ways to approach things can help children learn and think differently. It creates opportunities for them to build key skills for working on weaknesses and gaining new strengths.

There are a range of factors that can determine innate resilience. The DfE (2018) article 'Mental health and behaviour in schools' (https:// assets.publishing.service.gov.uk/government/uploads/system/uploads/ attachment_data/file/755135/Mental_health_and_behaviour_in_schools__. pdf) outlines the key elements of resilience in the child, the family, the community and the school. We paraphrase these below.

RESILIENCE IN THE CHILD

- Secure early relationships
- Being female
- Higher intelligence
- An easy temperament when an infant
- A positive attitude/a problem-solving approach

- Good communication skills
- Being a planner, having a belief in control
- Humour
- Religious faith.

RESILIENCE IN THE FAMILY

- At least one good parent–child relationship
- Affection
- Clear, firm and consistent discipline
- Support for education
- A supportive long-term relationship/an absence of severe discord.

RESILIENCE IN THE COMMUNITY

- A wide supportive network
- Good housing
- A high standard of living
- A high-morale school with positive policies for behaviour, attitudes and anti-bullying
- Opportunities for valued social roles
- A range of sport/leisure activities.

RESILIENCE IN SCHOOL

- Clear policies on behaviour and bullying
- An open-door policy for children to raise problems
- A whole-school approach to promoting good mental health
- Positive classroom management

- A sense of belonging
- Positive peer influence.

Taking these factors into account, there is no doubt that both nature and nurture play a part in developing, maintaining and supporting resilience. However, it is clear that school also plays a vital role in terms of the issues listed above. For this reason, it is important to develop a culture of resilience within school, to allow students a safe place to understand the concept of bouncing forwards.

Here also are some top tips for building resilience in the school setting:

1. Teach self-awareness and self-worth.
2. Look at challenges as new opportunities.
3. Encourage investigation wherever possible.
4. Praise the effort and not the person.
5. Help students to understand that success is getting what you want and happiness is liking what you get.
6. Mistakes will be made in the learning process but the key is to learn from them.
7. Teach your young people to trust their best instincts.
8. Provide examples of role models of resilience.
9. Don't just teach answers; teach students how to question.
10. Focus on a growth mindset.

TAKEAWAY

- Resilience isn't just 'bouncing back'. It's 'bouncing forward' – learning from challenges and finding the motivation to tackle the next one.

- Learning from setbacks can help children build self-awareness and self-advocacy skills.

- Allowing children to do things that are difficult – and even fail at them – can help build resilience.

CONCLUSION

You may have the best intentions, the best policies and procedures and an array of flexible approaches, but if the child won't work with you, you can't change their behaviour. It is vital that you form a connection with each of your children so that you can help support their behaviour.

NOTE IT DOWN

IF YOUR SYSTEMS ARE NOT WORKING, YOU WILL NEED TO REFLECT ON WHY THIS IS THE CASE. THE FOLLOWING PROBLEM-SOLVING EXERCISE SHOULD HELP THE SITUATION.

PROBLEM-SOLVING AUDIT

WHEN DO THE PROBLEMS OCCUR? (TIME OF DAY, SPECIFIC SITUATIONS)

WHAT ARE THE TRIGGERS (INTERACTION WITH OTHERS, BOREDOM, PARTICULAR TASKS)?

IN CONFRONTATION, HOW DOES HE/SHE REACT?

IN WHAT WAY DOES YOUR RESPONSE TO THE CHILD AFFECT THE OUTCOME?

WHAT SEEMS TO HAVE A POSITIVE AFFECT (YOUR APPROACH, HUMOUR, A CHANGE OF TASK)?

WHAT DID THE ABOVE EXERCISE TELL YOU? DID IT HELP YOU IDENTIFY SPECIFIC ISSUES THAT YOU MAY BE ABLE TO ACT ON, AND WILL YOU BE ABLE TO TRY SOMETHING DIFFERENT TO PREVENT THE SITUATION HAPPENING AGAIN?

SUMMARY

Any suggestions and strategies made in this book are a result of situations I have experienced over the years. My hope is that these thoughts and ideas, along with the activities and reflections, will support you in your own teaching journey and nudge you to discover your own ability to affect change in your practice.

Remember: behaviour is a message.

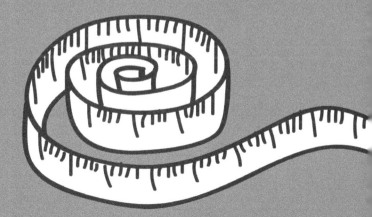

REFERENCES

Department for Education (DfE) (2015) 'Keeping children safe in education'. Available at: www.gov.uk/government/publications/keeping-children-safe-in-education--2 (accessed 21 May 2020).

Department for Education (DfE) (2018) 'Mental health and behaviour in schools'. Available at: https://assets.publishing.service.gov.uk/government/uploads/system/uploads/attachment_data/file/755135/Mental_health_and_behaviour_in_schools__.pdf (accessed 21 May 2020).

Long, R. (2016) NASEN annual conference, Reebok Stadium, Bolton.

Mehrabian, A. (1971) *Silent Messages*. Belmont, CA: Wadsworth.

Miller, L. (2011) *Mood Mapping: Plot your way to emotional health and happiness*. Emmaus, PA: Rodale.

Misteil, S. (1997) *Communicator's Pocketbook*. Aresford, Hants: Laurel House.

Oxford English Dictionary (OED) (2020) 'Behaviour', in OED. Oxford: Oxford University Press.

Rogers, B. (1997) *Cracking the Hard Class*. London: Paul Chapman Publishing.

INDEX